Tolerance

Celebrating Differences

by Robert Wandberg, PhD

Consultants:
Roberta Brack Kaufman, EdD
Dean, College of Education
Concordia University
St. Paul, Minnesota

Millie Shepich, MPH, CHES
Health Educator and District Health Coordinator
Waubonsie Valley High School
Aurora, Illinois

Roderick W. Franks, MA
Licensed Psychologist, Certified Mediator
Minneapolis, Minnesota

LifeMatters
an imprint of Capstone Press
Mankato, Minnesota

Thank you to the students of the Hennepin County Home School, who provided valuable feedback for the direction this book has taken.

LifeMatters Books are published by Capstone Press
PO Box 669 • 151 Good Counsel Drive • Mankato, Minnesota 56002
http://www.capstone-press.com

Printed in the United States of America

Library of Congress Cataloging-in-Publication Data
Wandberg, Robert.
      Tolerance: celebrating differences / by Robert Wandberg.
          p.   cm. — (Life skills)
      Includes bibliographical references and index.
      ISBN 0-7368-1021-8
      1. Toleration—Juvenile literature. 2. Prejudices—Juvenile literature. 3. Hate groups—Juvenile literature. 4. Pluralism (Social sciences)—Juvenile literature. 5. Pluralism (Social sciences)—United States—Juvenile literature. [1. Toleration. 2. Prejudices. 3. Hate groups. 4. Hate crimes.]
      I. Title. II. Series.
      HM1271 .W36 2002
      303.3´85—dc21   2001001754
                                         CIP

Summary: Describes tolerance and its importance in today's society. Discusses various aspects of tolerance, intolerance, and discrimination, including hate groups and hate crimes. Offers many how-to suggestions for increasing tolerance in oneself and others.

Staff Credits
Charles Pederson, editor; Adam Lazar, designer; Kim Danger, photo researcher

Photo Credits
Cover: ©Tim Yoon
Artville/© Claire Alaska, 17
Photo Network, 52/©Tom McCarthy, 8; ©Mark Newman, 11; ©Randy Taylor, 32; ©Esbin-Anderson, 35; ©John Sanford, 47; ©Myrleen Ferguson Cate, 50, 54; ©Myrleen Cate, 59
Photri, Inc, 21/©Frank Siteman, 7; ©DiRosa, 22
©Tim Yoon/5, 19, 29, 37, 49
Visuals Unlimited/©Charles Sanders, 30; ©SIU, 41

Table of Contents

Chapter Overview

Social tolerance is the ability to respect other people's beliefs, characteristics, and behavior.

Prejudice is negative feelings and thoughts about other people. It is learned and may result from fear. Discrimination is actions based on prejudice.

A continuing, irrational fear of an object, activity, or situation is called a phobia. People with a phobia may go out of their way to avoid the object of their phobia.

A self-assessment can help you decide what some of your prejudices are.

Another way to understand social tolerance is by looking at physical tolerance.

CHAPTER 1

What Is Tolerance?

Have you ever eaten food from another culture? Have you ever discussed religion with someone of a faith different from yours? Do you have friends whose skin color is not the same as yours? These are all examples of **ToleranceMatters,** which examines these differences. This chapter will describe different aspects of tolerance.

Social Tolerance: What Does That Mean?

Social tolerance is the ability to recognize and respect other people's beliefs, characteristics, and behavior. It starts with you. Social tolerance involves patience, control, communication, understanding, critical thinking, and honesty. It doesn't mean you must put up with other people's behavior or attitude if you disagree with it. It doesn't mean you may not try to change someone else's behavior or attitude. But it's the way in which you try to change it that is important. The key to tolerance is respect for others. It leads you to try to change their behavior in a respectful way.

"I can't stand people who are intolerant!"—Marge, age 14

Lucia, Age 15

"Mom!" called Lucia as she charged through the door after school. "We're studying tolerance this week in health class. I'm supposed to think of three things I'm intolerant about and how I could change them. I can't even think of one."

"Really?" asked Lucia's mom. "How about your brother's decision to join the army? You haven't spoken to him since he made up his mind to sign up."

"But it's so stupid that he wants to learn how to kill people!" cried Lucia.

"That's not very respectful, Lucia," said her mom. "You haven't even asked him why he decided to join. And I can think of better ways to try to change his mind than calling his decision 'stupid.'"

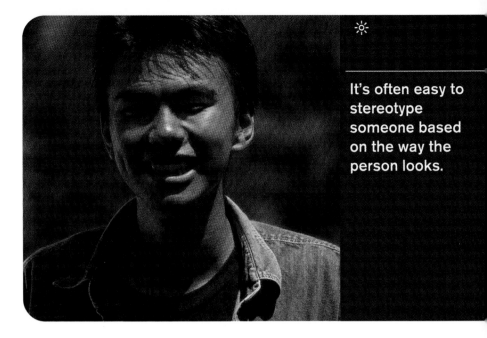

It's often easy to stereotype someone based on the way the person looks.

Prejudice

Prejudice is when people judge others without enough information. The negative feelings of prejudice have no basis in fact or are based on stereotypes. A stereotype is an oversimplified belief about an entire group of people. For example, someone may believe all Japanese people are good with computers. That's a stereotype. Some Japanese people are good with computers, some aren't.

Being tolerant can be difficult. It may involve feeling uncomfortable or awkward at times, and no one likes that. It might seem easier just to avoid those feelings and not have to think too much. People sometimes develop negative feelings about other individuals or groups because of this. These feelings may include hostility, suspicion, or hatred. These negative feelings can lead to prejudice.

People aren't born with prejudices. Prejudice is a learned attitude.

People aren't prejudiced when they are born. They learn behavior that unfairly prejudges people. It can be learned at home, in school, from friends, during sports activities, and in neighborhoods. Jobs, churches, music, TV, radio, advertisements, jokes, and movies may communicate prejudice.

Prejudice may result from a lack of understanding, which can lead to fear. Fear is often the basis of violence and hate crimes, which may include physical attacks and property damage. Hate crimes are motivated by prejudice against age, religion, race, or sexual orientation. Hate crimes sometimes are called bias crimes. Chapter 3 discusses hate crimes and hate groups.

Prejudice is different from dislike. You like or dislike someone based on knowing that person. You may, however, be prejudiced against a person or group without any personal knowledge of that person or group.

Discrimination

Prejudice is an attitude. Discrimination is the action that is based on prejudice. Discrimination distinguishes, isolates, or separates individuals or groups. It may involve avoiding, excluding, or verbally or physically abusing other people.

Many terms associated with prejudice and discrimination end with the letters *-ism*. Such terms usually imply that a more powerful group is acting against a less powerful group. For example, *ageism* is prejudice against people because of their age. *Sexism* is prejudice against people because they are male or female. *Racism* is prejudice against certain races or cultures. *Heterosexism* is prejudice against people who are bisexual or homosexual. Homosexual people are sexually attracted to others of the same gender. Bisexual people are sexually attracted to both males and females.

The word *phobia* comes from the Greek word *phobos*, which means "fear."

Phobias

A prejudice may become a phobia—a persistent and irrational fear of an object, activity, or situation. Persistent means continuous or ongoing. Irrational means unreasonable or unrealistic.

Some common phobias include the fear of insects, flying, crowds, enclosed places, snakes, and water. Some fears are normal in certain situations. For example, many people are afraid to speak before groups. When the fear becomes irrational and uncontrollable, it's considered a phobia. The fear is real, but phobias don't represent a real danger.

Some people may have a phobia of certain groups of people. They may go out of their way to avoid such people. For example, some people in our culture have phobias about people with a different skin color.

Social tolerance is about people. Socially tolerant people respect others. This helps them have healthy and positive relationships with people of all ages and cultures. Socially tolerant people often are fun to be with, are good listeners, and are willing to help in time of need. These are all qualities that most of us have to a degree and all of us can continue to develop.

Phobias are persistent, irrational fears. Many people have a phobia about snakes.

Recognizing My Prejudices: A Self-Assessment

Self-assessments are tests that help people know themselves better. There are many kinds of self-assessments. Some explore attitudes or behavior. Some look at risks for certain diseases such as cancer. Self-assessments can help you see how you're changing. The key to self-assessments is that only you interpret the information. This allows you to be completely honest in your answers.

Recognizing and accepting your own talents, abilities, and limitations helps you increase your self-esteem. People with strong self-esteem are less likely to put down other people. People with low self-esteem may put down others in an attempt to feel better about themselves. In this way, low self-esteem may lead to discrimination. Take the quick self-assessment on the following pages to see how tolerant your behaviors are.

My Tolerance Behaviors

Read items 1–18 below. On a separate piece of paper, write the answer for each item that best describes you. Use this scale:

3 = Almost always   2 = Sometimes   1 = Hardly ever

	3	2	1
1. I recognize the qualities in other people that make them different, unique, and special.	3	2	1
2. I challenge stereotypes that I hear and see.	3	2	1
3. I encourage people to feel good about themselves.	3	2	1
4. I avoid using hurtful words.	3	2	1
5. I try to cooperate with, respect, and work well with all people.	3	2	1
6. I read books that show diverse people.	3	2	1
7. I learn about different holiday customs.	3	2	1
8. I can count to 10 in several different languages.	3	2	1
9. I can empathize with others' feelings. This means I can understand their feelings and experiences.	3	2	1

10. I avoid telling prejudiced jokes.	**3**	**2**	**1**
11. I avoid laughing at jokes or negative comments about others.	**3**	**2**	**1**
12. I avoid buying games, CDs, or other products that reinforce stereotypes.	**3**	**2**	**1**
13. I attend events that celebrate cultures other than my own.	**3**	**2**	**1**
14. I watch travel videos about other countries.	**3**	**2**	**1**
15. I correspond with pen pals.	**3**	**2**	**1**
16. I enjoy music and art from different countries.	**3**	**2**	**1**
17. I spend time with students from other cultures and backgrounds.	**3**	**2**	**1**
18. I recognize stereotypes, racism, sexism, and other forms of prejudice and discrimination.	**3**	**2**	**1**

The closer your score is to 54, the more tolerantly you probably behave. Items on which you scored 1 or 2 may suggest areas for personal growth.

DID YOU KNOW?

The medical sense of the word *immunity* dates back to about 1879.

The Physical Side of Tolerance

The term *tolerance* in this book applies to social tolerance. Tolerance, however, has a physical aspect, as well. This is a body's ability to resist or survive infection and disease. Looking at physical tolerance can help you to understand social tolerance.

Protective Systems

The key to social tolerance is information. When we receive correct, accurate information about other people, our tolerance usually is increased. When working properly, our information system creates an immunity from prejudice and discrimination.

Sometimes, however, our information system is ineffective. We may receive incorrect information. Then, we may fail to be tolerant. We may stereotype an individual or even discriminate against that person.

Our information system is similar to our immune system. This helps the body resist invading germs. When working properly, the immune system keeps us from getting sick. When germs invade the body, the immune system reacts quickly. Sometimes, it reacts so quickly that we aren't even aware that an infection occurred.

At other times, the immune system may take longer. Then we may get sick. The immune system may need several days to catch up and defeat the infection. Sometimes, the immune system can fail, as in the case of AIDS. This disease overwhelms the immune system of the body and can eventually lead to death.

Some diseases are chronic. They develop over a long period of time. These diseases aren't infectious or communicable. This means you can't catch them from another person. Cancer, heart disease, arthritis, and high blood pressure are chronic diseases. Many chronic diseases result from a person's lifestyle choices. This includes choices about such behaviors as eating, smoking, or exercising. Most people with infectious diseases recover completely. Many people with chronic diseases remain ill for long periods of time.

Keeping Your Systems Healthy

Here are four ways to help keep your immune system healthy.

1. Eat a healthy, balanced diet. Each day, eat the following to strengthen your immune system:

2 to 3 servings of milk, yogurt, or cheese

2 to 3 servings of meat, poultry, fish, beans, eggs, or nuts

3 to 5 servings of vegetables

2 to 4 servings of fruits

6 to 11 servings of bread, cereal, rice, or pasta

Few, if any, servings of fats, oils, and sweets

2. Be positive. Medical professionals are continuing to better understand the mind-body connection. Some people believe that positive thinking may boost your immune system. Wouldn't it be great if you could laugh away a cold, chicken pox, or even athlete's foot?

3. Sleep. Make sure you get enough sleep and rest. Although people have varying needs, most teens should sleep at least eight hours each night.

4. Exercise. At least 20 minutes of continuous exercise several times a week will strengthen your immune system.

Keeping our information systems healthy is a way to increase our immunity against intolerance. We can make positive lifestyle choices to increase our tolerance of others. We can also be careful not to pass on unhealthy information to others. Here are three ways to keep your information systems healthy.

1. Learn to evaluate information critically. Teachers, librarians, and other trained adults can help you find accurate information. Always try to find information in more than one place. Be suspicious of information that comes from only one source.

2. Learn to locate accurate information. There are many sources of information, such as books, Internet sites, and toll-free phone numbers. Unless you know the source is respected or knowledgeable, you can't know for sure that the information is accurate. For example, the Centers for Disease Control and Prevention (CDC) is likely to provide high-quality, accurate information. An Internet site named "Daffy's Race Page" may not. A rumor that your friend heard also might not be accurate.

3. Learn what influences you toward prejudice and discrimination. Humor, false statistics, or statements from famous people may try to convince you that prejudiced behavior is acceptable. Beliefs that your best friend has might have a big influence on you but be incorrect or intolerant.

Keeping our information and immune systems healthy is a way to increase tolerance of others.

Points to Consider: ToleranceMatters

What does the word *tolerance* mean to you?

How do you think prejudice is learned? Give some examples from school, music, TV, or your community.

Can a person be tolerant and discriminatory? Explain your answer.

Chapter Overview

Intolerance has a long history in the world. Many immigrants have been able to make it in the "melting pot." Nonetheless, some people believe the United States should be called a "salad bowl."

It may be hard to know if you're being tolerant or intolerant. One way to tell that you're being tolerant is by acting with respect.

Developing your ethics can help keep you tolerant. Ethics that many people worldwide seek are called universal ethics. Ten clues can help tell you if your action was right or wrong.

Intolerance affects everyone. It can become a vicious circle that reinforces itself.

Openness

CHAPTER 2

The Importance of Tolerance

What's so important about tolerance, anyway? People in the United States and Canada come from many backgrounds. For all these people to live in harmony, they need tolerance. When people have been intolerant, we've seen riots and crimes take place. This chapter discusses **HarmonyMatters,** in which people of widely different backgrounds can get along together.

The U.S. Department of Labor estimates that by 2005, nearly half of all new workers will be women. Almost one-third of all new workers will be nonwhite.

A Brief Look at Intolerance

As in many places, intolerance has a long history in North America. For example, France and Spain were prominent in settling parts of North America. Many of their explorers and others were not tolerant of the native inhabitants.

Later, British citizens began arriving to establish colonies. Residents of these early colonies in America were mostly from Great Britain. Although there were many differences among these British groups, they were largely homogeneous. That is, they were alike in many ways, especially in language, history, customs, and appearance.

In the 1800s and early 1900s, many people came to the United States from European countries other than Great Britain. These groups of immigrants became frequent targets of intolerance by the majority group. Immigrants are people who move from one country to live permanently in another. They were often poor, didn't speak English well, and lived in easily identified areas.

With time, most European immigrants became part of the white majority. The immigrants often took on the character of the culture around them and fit in. This process of fitting in is often called the "melting pot."

Immigrants to North America have been frequent targets of intolerance.

However, many other people haven't considered themselves part of this melting pot. They may have had no desire to become like the majority group. African Americans, Central and South Americans, American Indians, and Asian groups, for example, have distinctive physical characteristics and cultural traditions. For example, African Americans have skin that often is darker than the skin of people from other groups. The majority group might see such characteristics as negative. This prejudice sometimes has kept individuals from taking full part in society.

Additionally, there has been a recent shift in immigration patterns. More immigrants come from Asian areas or from Mexico, for example, than from Europe. As time passes, the majority group will probably become a minority group itself. Some people call today's society a "salad bowl" rather than melting pot. This means that many different people make up the nation without having to be like each other. For racial, religious, and other kinds of harmony among people, tolerance will be even more necessary in the future.

Being respectful is important if you disagree with someone else's belief.

Tolerance in a Complicated World

You may be wondering how to tell if you're being tolerant or intolerant. For example, does tolerance mean you simply must accept all behaviors, even those you disagree with strongly? How can you know where to draw the line?

Respect for others is important. Even if you'd like to change someone's belief or behavior, you must be respectful. Two people may disagree about something that's important to each of them. But each must be respectful of the other's beliefs.

Try these quick techniques to judge yourself.

Golden rule: Treat others as you would like to be treated. If you aren't treating others that way, you may want to rethink your behavior. For example, you may be frustrated with someone who doesn't seem as smart as you. How could you approach the situation following the golden rule?

Parent on your shoulder: Behave as if a parent or other adult were in the room. For example, imagine you were considering making fun of someone's religion. If you aren't comfortable with the thought of a respected adult watching you, your behavior probably isn't right.

Publicity: Imagine your behavior is reported in the newspapers. Say you want to change a school rule that seems unfair. If you'd be embarrassed by a report of your actions to change the rule, you probably should try something else.

Ethics and Tolerance

Ethics also play a part in tolerance. Ethics are standards of right and wrong that guide a person's thinking and behavior.

Many societies, religions, and cultures worldwide seek to follow a common set of ethics. These ideas are universal ethics. They include responsibility, caring, fairness, respect, citizenship, and trustworthiness. These ideas can lead to specific behaviors. For example, the idea of fairness may lead you to protest against racially motivated crimes. Responsibility may lead you to point out prejudiced language rather than wait for someone else to do it.

Ethical behaviors are based on actions that can be defended, are logical, and that others understand. This means people have reasons for their actions. However, without ethics, there wouldn't be any consistent standards by which to judge people's behavior.

Ten Confirming Clues

Your feelings are sometimes a guide to knowing whether your action is right or wrong. However, you can't count only on your feelings in every situation. You still may wonder about your actions. The following 10 confirming clues can help you feel confident that you have done the right thing. Answer yes or no to each question. The more times you answer yes, the more sure you can be that you probably made the right choice.

1. My action was safe.

2. My action was legal.

3. My action was respectful of me and other people.

4. My action was healthy.

5. My action helped another person.

6. My action was based on knowledge, as well as emotion.

7. My action felt good.

8. My action felt right.

9. My action showed good character.

10. I'd take the same action again if I had the chance.

Tolerance in general has a good effect on people. Intolerance affects people, too, in a negative way, both physically and mentally.

"When you're told every single day for four hundred years that you're subhuman, when you rob people of their self-worth, knowledge, and history, there's nothing worse you can do."
–Spike Lee, American filmmaker

The Effects of Intolerance

Through the years, many groups have been the targets of discrimination and hate. For example, American Indians have been frequent targets of intolerance. The U.S. government conducted many wars against American Indians. Many have been forced to live on reservations. This amounts to several hundred years of prejudice and discrimination directed at this group alone. Many other groups also have had to deal with intolerance.

The most obvious physical effect of intolerance is violence. However, even intolerance that doesn't result in physical harm can cause a physical reaction. Have you ever been nervous about something and felt a headache or stomachache? So has Joon.

At Joon's school, someone painted messages on his locker that threatened Chinese people. Joon is Chinese, and the words frightened him. He's had a bad stomachache since then. It went away once his mother said he could stay home from school. But she's already said he has to go back tomorrow. "You've missed too much homework," she says. That night, Joon feels so sick he actually throws up. Maybe now his mother will let him stay home one more day.

Joon feels terrified, and his illness may be a reaction to stress. Discriminatory name-calling, threats, and vandalism such as graffiti often are intended to produce fear and insecurity. Graffiti is drawing or writing on a public surface. Feelings of fear can cause a person to experience physical illness such as Joon's.

Prejudice and discrimination can affect people in other ways. One reaction may be self-hatred and the denial of one's background. Another reaction is anger. However, anger sometimes can lead to positive change. For example, Martin Luther King, Jr., was angry about the treatment of African Americans in the United States. He focused his anger on creating positive change. His work helped change laws that discriminated against African Americans.

Intolerance: A Vicious Circle

Discrimination and prejudice often are based on fear and ignorance. Think about what happens when you're afraid of something. Say your friend said she overheard the new physical education teacher yelling at students who couldn't do pull-ups. The teacher did this in front of the whole class, your friend says. You know that you can't do pull-ups.

You've never talked with this teacher. You don't know anyone who has had a class with her. But you're afraid and will do nearly anything to avoid taking her class. You've made some prejudiced decisions based on fear. Because you're afraid, you may never allow yourself to know this teacher. You even might decide that all physical education teachers are scary.

The fear may become stronger and prejudice may grow if you don't try to find the truth. You even may tell others what your friend said, which was a rumor and not fact. The prejudice continues.

Points to Consider: HarmonyMatters

Which do you think is more accurate for your school, the "melting pot" or the "salad bowl"? Why?

Page 23 mentions three techniques to decide whether an action was ethical. Which of them might work for you? Explain.

Do you believe tolerance is important? Why or why not?

Chapter Overview

Our society is made up of people from many backgrounds. Disagreements and misunderstandings are bound to happen. An attitude of hate is one possible result of these disagreements. Stereotypes may reinforce hate.

Hate crimes are aimed at people's race, religion, gender, ethnic group, or sexual orientation. The number of hate crimes has risen over the last few years.

Members of hate groups feel important, powerful, and wanted because they make victims of other people. Hate groups often try to recruit teens.

The Internet has given hate groups an inexpensive yet effective way to spread their message of fear. However, many other groups oppose hate groups and their activities and promote tolerance.

CHAPTER 3

Hate Crimes and Hate Groups

Hatred of people based only on a group they belong to might be the worst kind of intolerance. It might seem unreasonable to be so full of hate toward someone you don't really know. Yet many groups and criminal acts are based just on that. This chapter will introduce **HateMatters** and look at hate crimes and some groups that hate.

Members of racial and ethnic groups may become victims of hate. American Indians have frequently been targets.

What Is Hate?

North America has people of every description. Our differences are bound to lead to disagreements and misunderstandings. Hate is one possible result.

Hate is an attitude. Often, it's based simply on differences. Hate is destructive. It can destroy a person by twisting his or her thoughts about other people. It can destroy the hated person's feelings of physical and emotional security and self-esteem.

Stereotypes are sometimes the reason behind ignorance and hate. When applied to people, stereotypes at best often lead to thoughtless behavior and attitudes. At worst, they can lead to hate or even violence.

Darryl, Age 16

"Things were just fine at school until the Mexicans started arriving. First, it was one family. Then some of their relatives moved to town. Then some more. Pretty soon, there was a whole bunch of them. They didn't make any effort to fit in. They just sat in their houses and did everything the way they did it in Mexico. I don't know why I'm supposed to understand them. They're the ones who are strangers here. They should be understanding us."

What About Hate Crimes?

Hate sometimes leads to crimes against a person based only on a group they are part of. These are called hate crimes. They are motivated by a person's race, religion, gender, ethnicity, or sexual orientation. Hate crimes may include hate mail, physical attacks, threatening phone calls, or destruction of property. Different states and Canadian provinces have different definitions of exactly what a hate crime is.

Immigrants may be targets of hate crimes because they often are easy to identify. They may dress or talk differently from others in an area. They may have a hard time getting the help they need after a hate crime.

Members of racial and ethnic groups are common victims of hate. In the United States and Canada, citizens of African background are the most common targets of hate crimes. About 60 percent of hate crimes are against people of African American background.

Many religious groups have been attacked and discriminated against throughout history. Similar attacks continue in North America today. Jews are a common target. The FBI reports that about three-fourths of all hate crimes based on religion are against people of Jewish background.

In recent years, issues such as gay rights have provoked violence from people who fear homosexuality. The number of reported hate crimes against homosexual people has risen.

In fact, the number of reported hate crimes in the United States has risen over the last decade. This has occurred since the introduction of the Hate Crimes Statistics Act of 1990. This may be partly because the law has made people more aware of hate crimes. However, many experts believe that most hate crimes either are unreported or are mistakenly not reported as hate crimes.

One of the better-known hate groups in the United States is the Ku Klux Klan.

Hate Groups

Hate groups are just what their name says. They are groups of people whose hate unites them. There are many well-known hate groups such as the Ku Klux Klan, the Aryan Nations, and some skinhead groups. Many smaller groups exist, too.

You might wonder what attracts people to hate groups. One big draw is a feeling of belonging and importance. Many people feel that they don't fit in anywhere. They might be outsiders. Maybe they haven't been able to make a team, join a group, or get the grades they wanted. Hate groups can make people feel welcome and wanted in the group.

Teens especially often feel like misfits. That is one reason hate groups recruit their members from this age group. Some of these young people on their own might never consider committing crimes. But they may feel pressure to do whatever the group wants in order to fit in. Hate groups also can give young people a sense of power that they otherwise might not have. Symbols, music, and slogans of hate groups are meant to give their members a feeling of power. At the same time, they cause fear in their victims. These can be powerful lures for many young people.

As of 1999, the Intelligence Project of the Southern Poverty Law Center counted 457 active hate groups in the United States.

Hate and the Internet

The Internet has provided a means for millions of people to express their ideas. Many groups have taken advantage of this technology to spread their message of hate. They use it as an inexpensive but effective way to reach people with similar beliefs. They also hope to bring people to their way of thinking.

Fortunately, other groups strongly oppose hate groups and their messages. These anti-hate groups keep track of hate groups and their Internet activities. The Anti-Defamation League (ADL) and the Southern Poverty Law Center (SPLC) are some of the larger groups. They provide information to counter the messages of the hate groups. Education is an important part of becoming more tolerant. These groups provide education about hate and its negative effects on people. They also have helped create laws against hate crimes.

"My neighbor used to say, 'You can't judge a book by its cover.' He always said that when someone commented on another person's appearance. I guess it's true about all people. Until you get to know them, you can't judge what they're like."
—Frank, age 18

Promoting Tolerance

Some people oppose hate on the Internet, and others promote tolerance in daily life. For example, a high school English teacher in California began a class called Promoting Tolerance Through Understanding. The class aims to make a practical difference in students' lives. It is also intended to solve some of the hate crimes that seem to plague many schools. The teacher, Joe Moros, is hopeful that schools all over North America will welcome such a practical approach.

Often, when hate incidents or hate crimes occur, the victims are left to speak out for themselves. This shouldn't be the case. If one group is attacked, all people need to respond. Efforts such as Moros's help people to recognize their dependence on each other.

Colleen, Age 15

"I was a good skinhead racist. I thought I had good reasons to hate blacks, Jews, Chicanos, everyone. After my arrest for vandalizing a synagogue, I was ordered to go to counseling. I only went to tell all my reasons for hating these people. But then I sat in the same room with them and listened to them. Suddenly, they weren't just Jews, whites, whatever. I had to start seeing them as people. The counselor's support and concern were important in helping me, too."

Many skinheads hate all kinds of people who aren't in their group.

Points to Consider: HateMatters

How would you feel if a member of a hate group asked you to join the group? How could you respond?

How might you help a friend who received hate mail?

Think about how you handle anger and conflict. Is it a positive way? How could you handle your anger more positively?

Chapter Overview

Tolerance is needed for people to get along. There is some question whether it can go too far.

Religion and race are two areas where questions about tolerance may arise.

Many people have strong feelings about the right and wrong of AIDS research and animal experimentation.

Abortion and carrying weapons in school are other important issues in which tolerance plays a large role.

CHAPTER 4 ⬡

The Limits of Tolerance

Most people agree that tolerance is needed for people to live together peacefully. People speak different languages. They have different religious beliefs and cultural backgrounds. They have different skills and abilities. About half of us are female, half are male. Yet, while most agree on the importance of tolerance, it takes hard work. Throughout history, many conflicts have been the direct result of intolerance.

Can tolerance go too far? Can efforts to achieve tolerance result in intolerance? How do laws affect tolerance? This chapter will explore these complicated questions of **TangledMatters.**

Tolerance or Intolerance?

Andy and Jason, Age 14

Andy and Jason were walking home from school. Passing a church, they noticed some kids spray-painting negative statements about religion on it. "Hey, Andy," said Jason. "Look at those kids! They're wrecking that church! I'm calling the police."

"Wait a minute," said Jason. "Maybe you don't like those messages, but those kids have a right to say them. It's a free country, remember?"

Noel and Sheryl, Age 16

Noel was walking to class when he stopped short. He couldn't believe what he was overhearing. "Antony is the last person I'd ask to take notes for me," Sheryl was saying to her friend. "Everybody knows those people are lazy and dumb. He'd get everything wrong!" Noel felt his temper rising. He wheeled around and headed for the principal's office.

What Do You Think?

Imagine Andy decides to call the police. Is he failing to recognize and respect the attitudes and beliefs of the kids spray-painting the church? In other words, is he being intolerant? Why or why not? If Noel reports Sheryl to the principal, is he being intolerant? Why or why not?

These aren't easy questions to answer. The fictional case study that follows might make the issues even more complicated for you! But it may help you think about your own attitudes and beliefs.

FAST FACTS

The Centers for Disease Control and Prevention estimates that worldwide, 36.1 million people live with HIV/AIDS. Of these, 1.4 million are children younger than age 15. During 2000, AIDS caused the deaths of an estimated 3 million people, including 500,000 children younger than 15.

Case Study: Dr. Thomson's Research

Janet and Bruce were reading a medical article for a school report. The article was about Dr. Thomson's research into a cure for AIDS. Thomson's research could possibly save millions of lives.

However, the article said that Thomson intentionally injected healthy test subjects with the AIDS virus. These individuals had no history or record of HIV infection or AIDS. Thomson tried his new cures on them.

"That's terrible!" exclaimed Bruce. "How can he get away with that?" Janet agreed.

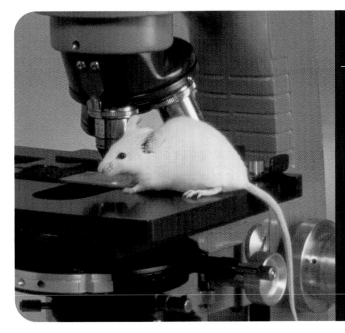

Medical research on animals has led to many important treatments. However, some people believe the research should be done without using animals.

Thomson stated that his research might reduce the pain and suffering of AIDS patients and their families. He said, "We can't wait for volunteers for trial treatment." Sometimes the trial cure didn't work. Those individuals were humanely killed and their body sent to a lab for more testing.

Then Janet and Bruce read that Thomson never used human beings in his research. He only used rats. The two felt relieved that people weren't being used. However, Janet said it's never okay to conduct medical experiments with animals. Bruce disagreed.

AT A GLANCE

Animals have been used in research for more than 2,000 years. In the 200s B.C., the natural philosopher Erisistratus of Alexandria used animals to study body functions.

This fictional case study brings up an interesting point. Many people have strong opinions about the use of animals in medical research. Some people want equal rights for all citizens. Organizations have formed seeking the same protection for animals. These groups often believe that there is no such thing as killing an animal in a humane manner.

On the other hand, some people support humane animal research. They say that the potential medical advances outweigh the suffering of individual animals.

Let's say you believe that it's acceptable to use animals in experiments. Should you tolerate the beliefs and actions of those who think that it's unacceptable? Some animal rights groups have broken laws to protect animals. For example, at the University of Minnesota in 1999, people broke into a research lab. They released pigeons, rats, mice, and lizards being used for research on brain cancer and other diseases. How tolerant of someone else's beliefs would you be? Is not accepting a view that opposes your own—that is, being intolerant of another's view—ever right or ethical?

Abortion and Weapons in School

Two issues that are frequently debated in our society are abortion and weapons in school.

Abortion

Few issues in our society are more controversial than abortion. This is the intentional ending of a pregnancy before birth.

Starting in colonial times, women in the United States could end a pregnancy up until they could feel the baby move. Following the Civil War, tougher abortion laws were passed. By 1900, most U.S. states didn't allow abortion except to save the mother's life.

In 1973, the U.S. Supreme Court declared that a woman has a Constitutional right to privacy. This includes the legal right to have an abortion.

Many people have strong feelings about abortion. Most believe in one of two positions. One is that a woman may decide whether to continue a pregnancy. Some people believe abortion is acceptable if the fetus, or unborn child, has severe physical or mental problems. Some people believe abortion is acceptable if a pregnancy results from rape or sexual intercourse among family members.

Many abortions in the United States are performed on women younger than age 25. Most abortions are performed on unmarried women. Most abortions are performed during the first 12 weeks of pregnancy.

Another position is that every fetus has a right to live and needs someone to stand up for those rights. Some people see abortion as the taking of an innocent life. People with this opinion define life as beginning at the moment when the baby begins to develop.

Groups that oppose abortion in the United States have used both peaceful and violent means to show their opinion. Is it unethical to oppose a legal practice? Are there appropriate ways to challenge a law? If so, what are they? What is your definition of when human life begins? Do you recognize and respect a definition different from yours? Would you be tolerant of someone who chooses a pregnancy option that you don't agree with? Can you disagree but still respect the person? Why or why not?

According to the CDC, nearly 10 percent of students have been threatened or injured with a weapon on school property. Another survey of high school students shows that about 1 of 20 students had carried a gun at least once during the 30 days before the survey.

Weapons in School

For learning to take place, schools must be safe. Students and teachers need to know that their school isn't a dangerous place. Unfortunately, tragedies involving guns and other weapons in schools continue to occur. Schools across North America are increasingly concerned about safety. The availability and use of weapons in school is a growing worry. As a student, you have the responsibility to report behaviors that threaten the safety of students and staff. Many potential school tragedies have been prevented because of alert, conscientious, and responsible students.

For this reason, many schools have a zero-tolerance policy for the possession of any weapon able to produce bodily harm or death. Schools with a zero-tolerance policy allow no guns, real or fake. Serious consequences result from breaking the policy.

It's estimated that by age 18, the average person has watched 32,000 murders and 40,000 attempted murders on TV.

In another recent case, a student brought a homemade model rocket to school. School weapons policy classified the toy as a weapon. Based on the policy, the school suspended him for the rest of the year. In another report, a second-grader was expelled from school after displaying a cap gun on a school bus. Should zero tolerance of weapons mean there's no room for schools to judge each case? Why or why not?

As you can see, there are no easy answers to the question "Are there limits to tolerance?" Only you know how to answer that question for yourself. Your answer depends on your thoughts and feelings on an issue, based on knowledge, respect, and personal ethics. Your answer could—and probably will—change, depending on the issue.

Many schools have zero-tolerance policies against any weapons in school.

Points to Consider: TangledMatters

Do you think there are limits to tolerance? Explain your answer.

In one story in this chapter, some people spray-painted a church. How do you feel about the witnesses' reactions? Would you feel differently if only words had been said and not spray-painted?

How could you find out more about any of the issues discussed in this chapter? Whom could you ask?

Chapter Overview

It's up to each person to set a good example of tolerance.

There are many ways to model tolerance at home, at school, and in the community.

We all need to pass on to children everything we have learned about tolerance. Prejudice can be unlearned, but it's best to start out right by learning tolerance.

Think for yourself about matters of tolerance as you would about anything else.

CHAPTER 5

⌂

Improve Your World

Hate and discrimination can be serious problems. It might seem tough to find ways to stand up to them. In this chapter, **ImprovementMatters** will illustrate ways to make a positive, healthy difference at school, at home, and in your community. Many teens feel that because they are only one person, they can't influence important issues. As you will read, you can take many actions that will make a difference.

You have the chance to be respectful and tolerant every day.

Setting a Good Example

As the saying goes, "Most people would rather see a sermon than hear one." Every day, you have the opportunity to model respectful behavior. Commit yourself to take personal responsibility to learn more about tolerance and to set a positive example of respectful behavior. Develop positive values about tolerance. Your values define for you what is good and bad, right and wrong. Your values guide your behavior. Seek challenges. Don't allow others to pressure you into behaviors that discriminate against others.

Amos, Age 13

"I used to look around and see lots of problems in my neighborhood. I thought, 'What can I do? I'm just one guy.' But it turns out that a single person can do a lot. I asked my dad if I could use some paint we had left over from painting the garage. Then I knocked on people's doors and asked if they would let me paint over some of the graffiti. It wasn't long before other people joined me."

Amos found out that making a difference can be as simple as having an idea. Following are several ways to act on your own ideas.

"Our lives begin to end the day we become silent about things that matter."—Martin Luther King, Jr.

Ways to Oppose Intolerance

There's a saying, "No individual snowflake ever felt any responsibility for an avalanche." But you can start your own avalanche against intolerance. There are dozens of ways you can make a difference whether at home, in school, or in the community. Ask trusted adults for help if you need it.

At Home

Identify your own personal heroes and positive role models.

Invite friends from different backgrounds to take part in your traditions and customs. Ask them about their customs.

Know enough information to reject harmful myths and stereotypes.

Know your ethnic background and proudly share it with others.

Read and encourage your family to read books about other cultures or by authors from backgrounds different from yours.

Speak out against jokes about people or groups. Silence sends the message that you agree.

Some schools encourage their students to paint over racist graffiti.

At School

Begin classroom discussions of terms such as *racism* or *stereotyping*. Post the definitions in a place that everyone can see.

Create a school flag that has symbols promoting diversity.

Form your own opinions about other people.

Ignore people who promote hate.

Interview teachers about their ethnic or racial background. Ask how that background influences their experiences.

Join an orientation program that helps all new students feel part of the school.

Organize an essay contest about how people have successfully opposed racism or prejudice. See if your school or community newspaper will publish the winners.

You may have thought about doing a group project to oppose hate and intolerance. Here are some ideas to get started.

1. Decide on a project. For example, you might want to create and display tolerance posters at school.

2. Make a plan. Decide who will do what and set deadlines for each task.

3. Get what you need. This includes getting materials and people. Don't forget about transportation, adult support, money, food, meeting space, and publicity.

4. Start your project. Do what you planned to do.

5. Check your progress. See if what you're doing is working. For example, have you created the posters by the date you set for completion?

6. Get the message out. Tell people what you're doing and ask for their help. Share successes with your school or local newspaper.

Paint over racist graffiti.

Suggest establishing a diversity club to promote harmony and mutual respect.

Research civil unrest from the time of slavery to the present day.

Take part in programs that match students from different schools or that match older students with younger student "buddies."

Tell school authorities or police about hate group activities at school.

Children need teens and adults to teach them to be tolerant of others.

In Your Community

Contribute letters to your local newspaper with themes of tolerance and understanding.

Make sure your public buildings are usable for all residents, including those with disabilities.

Research your town's diversity and compare it with other cities to understand your community better.

Serve on committees that raise awareness about prejudice.

Teaching Children

It's wonderful when each person takes responsibility today to reduce hate and promote tolerance among people. But what about in a year, or 10 years, or 30 years? Someone needs to carry on what you've started. That means children, whether they are ours or someone else's, need teachers. Children are our best hope for opposing hate and promoting understanding.

Prejudice and hatred are learned. While it's true that such attitudes can be unlearned, it's easier to start out right by teaching tolerance. It is up to each of us to teach children better ways.

Help each child feel special. Children with high self-esteem are more likely to be tolerant.

Help children recognize other people's feelings.

Point out and discuss discrimination with children when you see it. Children need to know that such behavior is unacceptable from either children or adults. Say, "Please don't talk that way around me or children."

Let children be with people from other groups. This helps people develop positive attitudes about each other.

Help children know that appearance or differences aren't the most important quality in friends. It's what's inside that counts the most.

Help children to have a response to different situations. Confronting friends and classmates can be especially hard. If someone is called a hurtful name, a child can say, "Don't call him that. Use his name." If the child is the target, she or he can say, "You don't like to be called names, and neither do I."

"Great spirits have always encountered violent opposition from mediocre [low ability] minds."
–Albert Einstein, scientist

Critical Thinking About Tolerance

You've learned about ways to view tolerance. Some of the issues presented may be confusing.

Critical thinking about the issues of tolerance is essential. Being a critical thinker means looking carefully at both sides. Do not automatically accept opinions about tolerance.

Using critical thinking skills can help you evaluate the claims and opinions of others. It will help you define and defend your beliefs. As a critical thinker, you will realize that your beliefs are based on a combination of scientific information, your judgment, and your ethics.

It's believed that Abraham Lincoln said, "I do not think much of a man who does not know more today than he did yesterday." To help yourself continue to learn every day, here are some guidelines to consider.

1. Question the reasons behind the sources of information. Find out who said it and why.

2. Define terms. Some statements may be true or false depending on how words are defined. For example, to say that being intolerant is bad for you depends on the definition of the word *intolerant.* It also depends on the issues involved.

3. Question assumptions, opinions, and theories in arguments. Just because "everyone knows" something is true does not make it true.

4. Don't oversimplify information. Some issues related to tolerance, discrimination, and prejudice are tangled.

"He that is good for making excuses is seldom good for anything else."—Benjamin Franklin, U.S. politician, writer, and inventor

A Final Thought

Martin Niemoeller was a German preacher during the 1930s and 1940s. He boldly spoke up against intolerance toward Jews and others. Here's what he thought the effect of keeping silent might be.

"In Germany they came first for the communists, and I didn't speak up because I wasn't a communist. Then they came for the Jews, and I didn't speak up because I wasn't a Jew. Then they came for the trade unionists, and I didn't speak up because I wasn't a trade unionist. Then they came for the Catholics, and I didn't speak up because I was a Protestant. Then they came for me, and by that time no one was left to speak up."

It's up to each of us to take a stand and practice tolerance. Don't stop with the ideas in this chapter. Brainstorm other ways to reduce prejudice and increase understanding and respect. Take the first step today.

Each individual must stand up and practice tolerance. Get started today.

Points to Consider: ImprovementMatters

Explain this statement: "Most people would rather see a sermon than hear one."

Which idea from the lists on pages 51–54 would be easiest to do at home? at school? in the community?

How do you think children feel when teens pay serious attention to them? Do you think it's important how children feel?

NOTE

At publication, all resources listed here were accurate and appropriate to the topics covered in this book. Addresses and phone numbers may change. When visiting Internet sites and links, use good judgment. Remember, never give personal information over the Internet.

Internet Sites

National MultiCultural Institute
www.nmci.org/links.htm
Links to many Internet sites on cultures and tolerance

Promoting Tolerance
www.teachtolerance.org
Information about starting a tolerance class in your school

University of Minnesota Human Rights Library—Peace and Activist Links
www1.umn.edu/humanrts/peace/peacelinks.html
Many links to groups that promote worldwide peace and justice

Anti-Defamation League (ADL)
823 United Nations Plaza
New York, NY 10017
www.adl.org
Information on hate groups and other forms of extremist behavior; puts on workshops, provides curriculums.

Josephson Institute of Ethics
4640 Admiralty Way, Suite 1001
Marina del Rey, CA 90292-6610
www.charactercounts.org
Information and resources about using ethics in everyday life

Southern Poverty Law Center (SPLC)
400 Washington Avenue
Montgomery, AL 36104
www.splcenter.org
Many resources on promoting tolerance and opposing prejudice, such as Klanwatch, which tracks racist hate groups; offers videos and *Teaching Tolerance* magazine.

For Further Reading

Duncan, Alice Faye. *The National Civil Rights Museum Celebrates Everyday People.* Mahwah, NJ: BridgeWater Books, 1995.

Garg, Samidha, and Jan Hardy. *Racism.* Austin, TX: Raintree Steck-Vaughn, 1997.

Tatum, Beverly Daniel. *"Why Are All the Black Kids Sitting Together in the Cafeteria?": And Other Conversations About Race.* New York: Basic Books, 1999.

Wandberg, Robert. *Conflict Resolution: Communication, Cooperation, Compromise.* Mankato, MN: Capstone, 2001.

Wandberg, Robert. *Ethics: Doing the Right Thing.* Mankato, MN: Capstone, 2001.

Glossary

discrimination (diss-krim-i-NAY-shuhn)—actions based on prejudice; discrimination distinguishes, isolates, or separates individuals or groups.

diversity (di-VUR-suh-tee)—variety

hate crime (HATE KRIME)—a crime motivated by prejudice against age, religion, race, or sexual orientation

heterosexism (het-ur-oh-SEKSS-izm)—prejudice against people who are bisexual or homosexual

immigrant (IM-uh-gruhnt)—a person who moves from one country to live permanently in another

minority (muh-NOR-uh-tee)—a particular group of people living among a larger group; minorities may be religious, ethnic, racial or other groups.

phobia (FOH-bee-uh)—persistent and irrational fear of an object, activity, or situation

prejudice (PREJ-uh-diss)—negative opinion or judgment about people based on a stereotype rather than individual qualities

racism (RAY-sizm)—prejudice against certain races or cultures

sexism (SEK-sizm)—prejudice against people because they are a particular gender

stereotype (STER-ee-oh-tipe)—an oversimplified belief about an entire group of people

tolerance (TOL-ur-uhnss)—the ability to recognize and respect other people's beliefs, characteristics, and behavior

Index

Index Continued